AH...
CHOO!

ABRAMS, NEW YORK

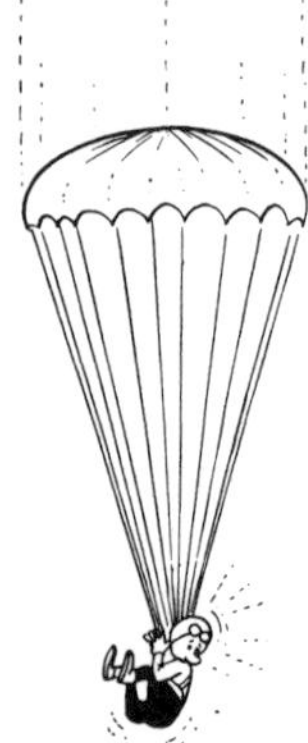

EDITOR: Charles Kochman
EDITORIAL ASSISTANT: Sofia Gutiérrez
DESIGNER: Galen Smith
PRODUCTION MANAGER: Jacqueline Poirier

Library of Congress Cataloging-in-Publication Data

Jaffee, Al.
[Tall tales. Selections]
Tall tales / by Al Jaffee ; introduction by Stephen Colbert.
p. cm.
Selection of comic strips originally published between 1957 and 1963.
ISBN 978-0-8109-7272-8
1. American wit and humor, Pictorial. I. Title.

NC1429.J34A4 2008
741.5'6973—dc22

2008004773

Published in 2008 by Abrams, an imprint of Harry N. Abrams, Inc.

Printed and bound in China
10 9 8 7 6 5 4 3 2 1

harry n. abrams, inc.
a subsidiary of La Martinière Groupe

115 West 18th Street
New York, NY 10011
www.hnabooks.com

TO JOYCE

ACKNOWLEDGMENTS

To Charlie Kochman, my editor and friend, for his creative guidance in every aspect of this project; to his assistant Sofia Gutiérrez for efficiently keeping everything on track; and to the late Harry Welker, editor of the Herald Tribune Syndicate, for helping to launch Tall Tales in many newspapers.

"I had dinner last night with Al Jaffee."

Four years ago, after I had, in fact, had dinner with Al, I tried the above sentence out on friends, family, and colleagues. I saw it as something like the acid test for gold. If the person I was bragging to melted with jealousy, I knew that they had misspent their childhood the same way I had: poring over Al's comics.

I certainly learned a lot from those drawings—a lot of dumb, dumb things. These days I make a living being professionally ridiculous, and pride myself on the ability to be an idiot on a moment's notice. I'm sure I owe some of that to Al. I certainly have to

credit him for whatever ability I have to give Snappy Answers and ask Stupid Questions.

He also taught me that it is not necessary to become a wise old man. Al is still a fool and, make no mistake, Al is old. How old? Brace yourself. Al is older than *MAD* Magazine. Yes, there was actually a time *before* he was a member of the "Usual Gang of Idiots." A time when Al Jaffee was a free-range moron. This book is a collection of cartoons from that misty past—a collection which proves that not only has Al always been funny, he's always been disturbed.

I'm so honored to be introducing this slender volume of wrongness. Plus, I can't wait to try this on my friends:

"Al Jaffee asked me to introduce his new book."

Not melting with jealousy?

I pity you.

I pity your well-spent youth.

Stephen Colbert
New York City
March 2008

STEPHEN COLBERT is a Peabody Award–winning American comedian, satirist, actor, and writer. He is the author of the #1 *New York Times* bestseller *I am America (And So Can You!).*

PREFACE

TALL TALES was created at a critical point in my professional career. Here's the not-so-tall tale of how it came about.

In the mid-1950s my friend Harvey Kurtzman created *MAD*, which he left in 1956 in order to produce a glossy rival version for Hugh Hefner (yes, he of *Playboy* magazine fame). I soon joined Kurtzman, Will Elder, Arnold Roth, and Jack Davis as the creative staff of the new publication. Unfortunately *Trump*, as it was called, bit the dust after only two issues.

Undeterred, Kurtzman decided that we all should publish another magazine, this time on our own. We scrambled for funds to get it started and in 1957 *Humbug* was born. After eleven fantastic (if I say so myself) issues, a shortage of money, along with terribly ineffective distribution forced us to draw the curtain on this effort as well.

Having been thrown back into the capricious world of freelance cartooning, I soon gave up eating in order to make ends meet. However, desperation (and hunger) often spurs creativity. After examining my options, I decided a syndicated comic strip offered not only economic security but would also be a great way to do the kind of cartooning that I enjoy doing. But getting a syndicate to take on a new creation was not so simple, I realized. I discovered that out of hundreds of thousands of submissions a year, perhaps one makes it. Deep down I knew it would be challenging to do this type of assignment seven days a week, fifty-two weeks each year. But for reasons even I don't understand, this was enough of a challenge that I decided to go for it!

I set about analyzing the comic strip business and discovered that newspaper space for cartoons was jealously guarded. The only way a new feature could break into the funny pages was by kicking someone else out. And when a comic strip was kicked out, the newspaper often was deluged with nasty letters from fans of the old strip. This was not encouraging. I realized that if I was to have a chance in this lottery, I'd have to create something truly unique.

The only thing I could think of was a comic feature that could fit into spaces that other comic features couldn't. After exploring every gimmick I could think of, I came up with the idea of a *vertical* format instead of the standard *horizontal* one—seven inches tall and one column wide. The natural title came to me: Tall Tales. It could be put on any page of the newspaper: the classified section, the editorial page, or anywhere else the editor wished to attract special attention.

Best of all, in this enlarged format I could create many gag situations by employing a "double take." In a seven-inch vertical space our eyes can't take in the entire area at once. As readers, we have a tendency to look at the strongest focal point first and then the secondary area. This dynamic allowed me to place the set-up for the joke in the first-glance area and pull the punch line with the second glance. In a few days time I had a batch big enough to submit to the New York Herald Tribune Syndicate. To my shock and surprise, they decided to distribute it. This was 1957. Looking back, that was a busy, productive year for me.

Another part of my plan was to do the feature in pantomime, that is to say, without any words. I'd always enjoyed the work of cartoonists who could communicate humor with their drawing alone. By making Tall Tales a silent strip, I reasoned it could be sold to publishers anywhere in the world without needing to be translated. Although the panels had no words in them, I did allow myself some universally understood symbols, sound effects, traffic signs, etc. The approach worked, and encouraged many publications in foreign countries to sign on as clients of Tall Tales.

Now, the one question that every cartoonist is asked above all others is, "Where do you get your ideas?" Doing three-hundred and sixty-five cartoons a year means you can't just pull them out of thin air (at least, I haven't been able to, but then again the ventilation in my studio isn't all that funny). Every cartoonist has his or her own particular way of coming up with gags. Mine is a kind of free association. I'll often sit down with books and magazines and newspapers—not to copy the work of others but rather to stimulate my imagination. For example, a picture of someone slipping on a banana peel might make me think of a skater slipping on ice, and an idea for a humorous situation would come to mind.

Through the years of working on Tall Tales I made some adjustments as the strip developed. For example, I didn't always follow the double-take formula. If I had an idea that was funny at a single glance, I'd do it.

To give the feature some continuity from day to day, I created a recurring character—Sidney Sneath—who appears throughout these pages. I incorporated Sidney as an observer, and used his reactions to the various situations in each panel as a proxy for the reader. (For any etymologists out there wondering, "Sneath" came from the name of a local real estate agency I'd pass on my way home, and I added "Sidney" for the alliteration.)

One adjustment to the strip was imposed on me, and it proved to be objectionable and the undoing of the feature. As you can imagine, syndicating internationally provided me with a steady income. One day a new executive at the Herald Tribune who was somewhat intellectually challenged informed me that "Americans don't like wordless cartoons," and insisted I add dialogue to my panels. I reluctantly acquiesced and, as a result, the words went in and my foreign clients went away. With this kind of meddling, the feature became an unpleasant chore and less and less successful. After six years, the syndicate and I parted company in 1963 (some 2,200 strips later).

In this book I've selected the best of the wordless early years. I have no snappy answer here, but I hope as you fold this in to your other reading, you enjoy these tall tales as much as I did in creating them.

Al Jaffee
New York City
December 2007

POLICE

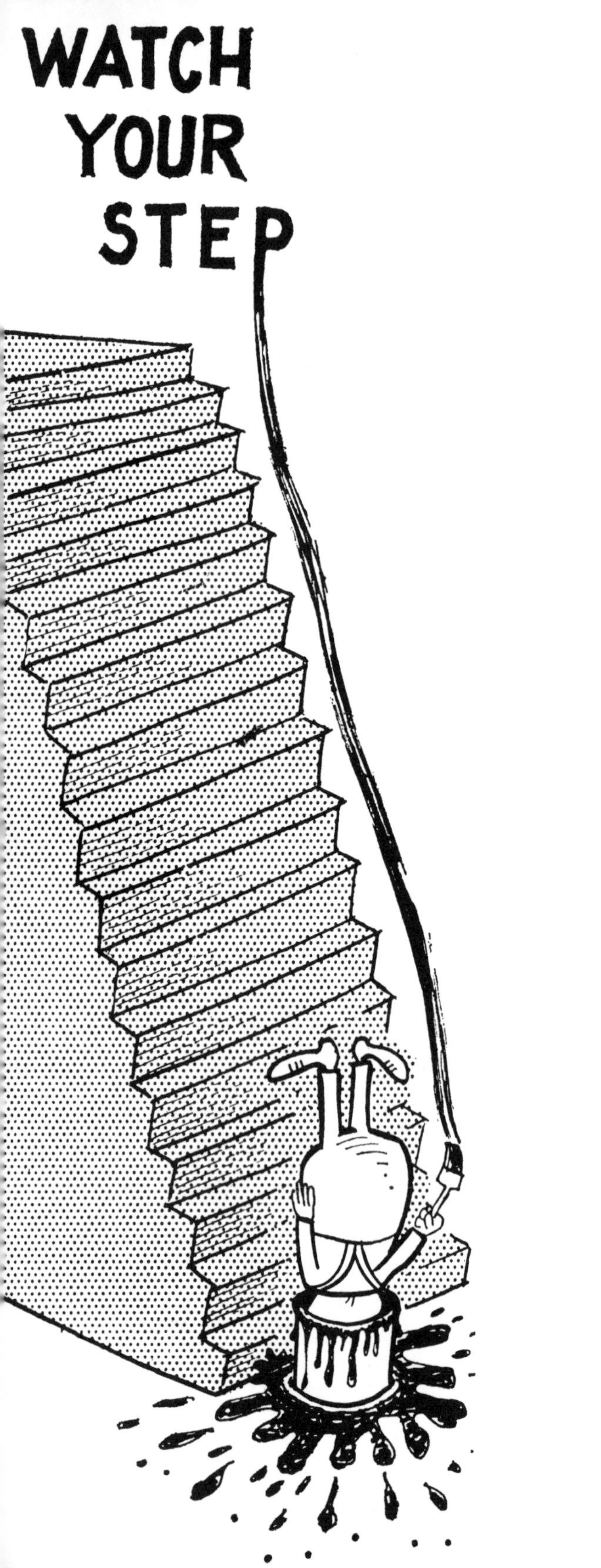
WATCH
YOUR
STEP

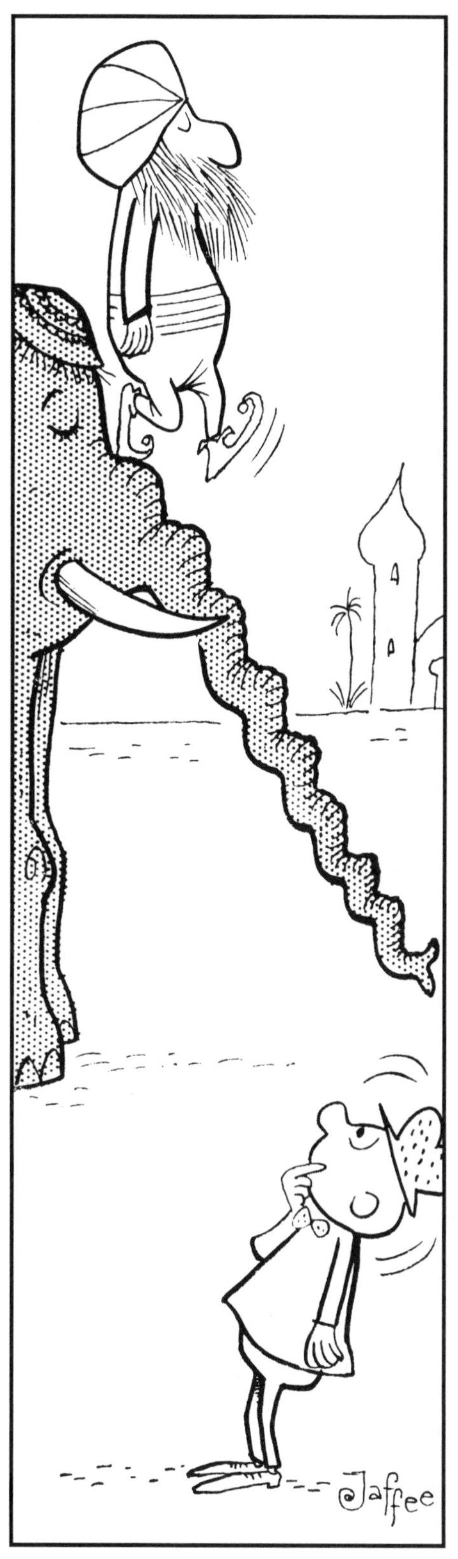
Jaffee

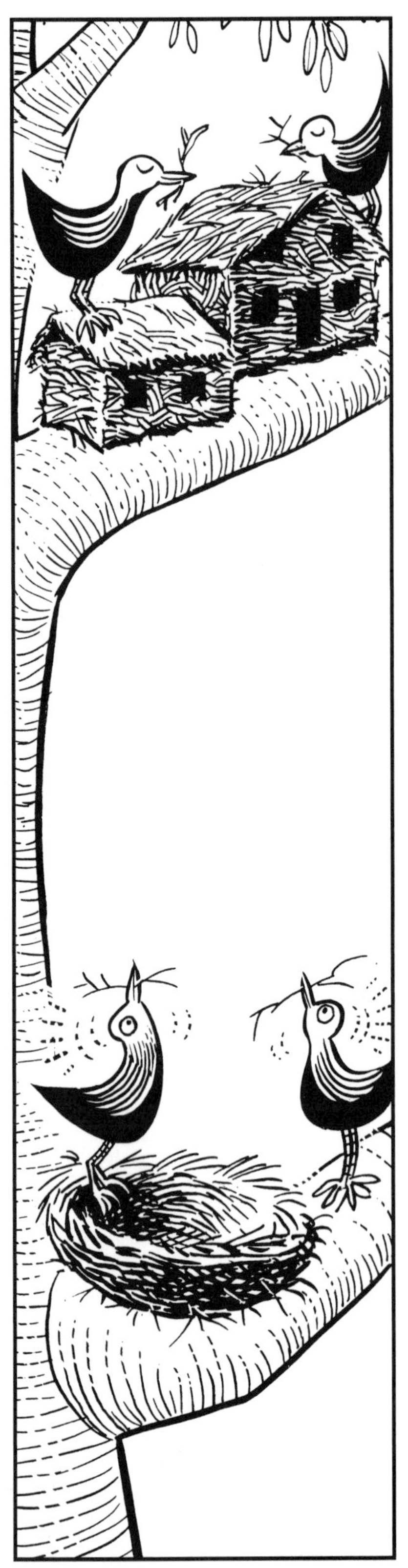

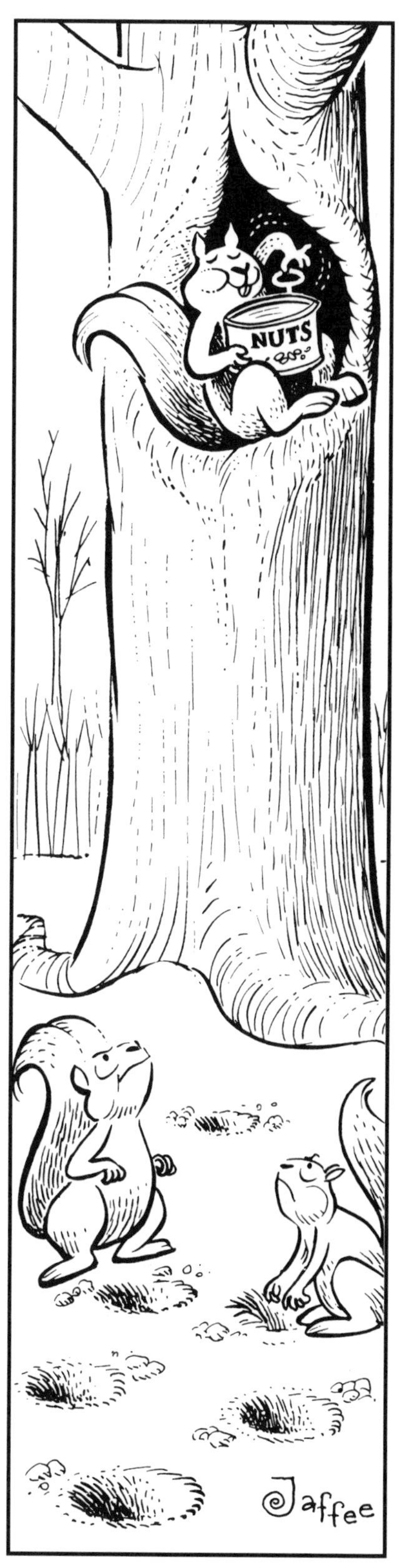
NUTS
Jaffee

BEAR
RIGHT

BEWARE
OF
DOG

Jaffee

JUST MARRIED
Jaffee

Jaffee

Jaffee

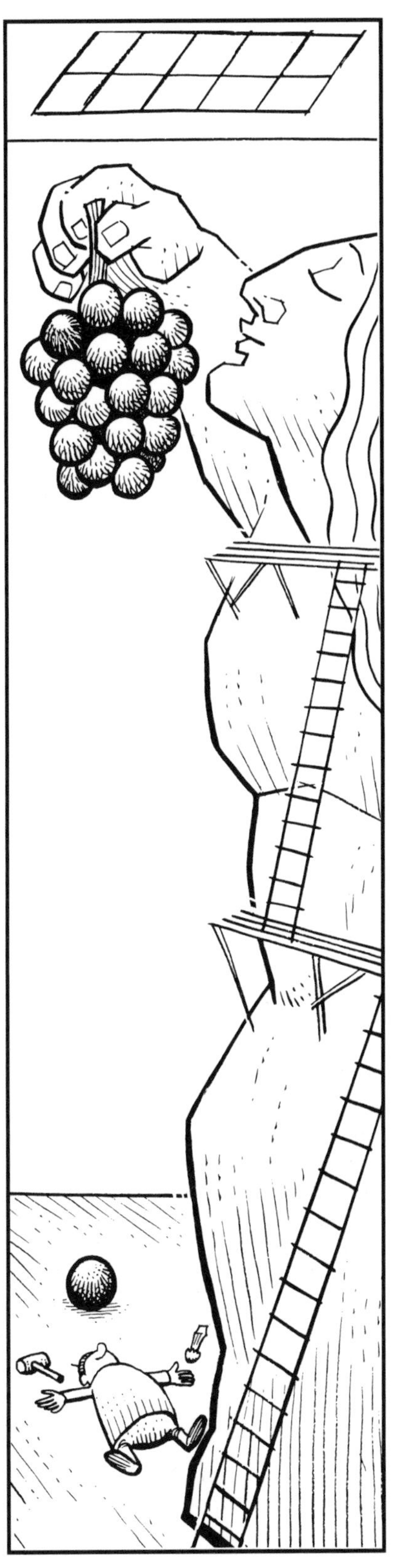

FOOD
CONCENTRATES
ADD WATER
BEFORE
USING
Jaffee

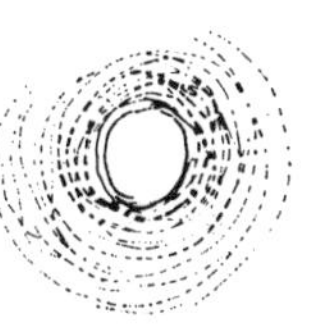
OASIS
MIRAGE
DANCING
GIRLS
MIRAGE

©Jaffee

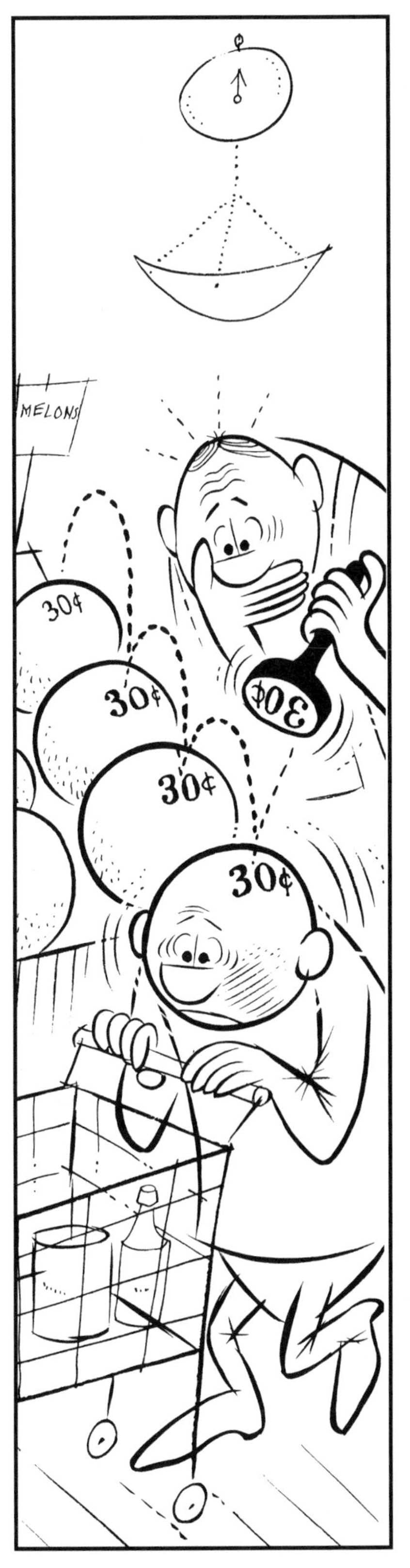
MELONS
30¢
30¢
30¢
30¢
30¢

ZZZZZz
Jaffee

©Jaffee

Jaffee

Jaffee

SAFETY FIRST
Jaffee

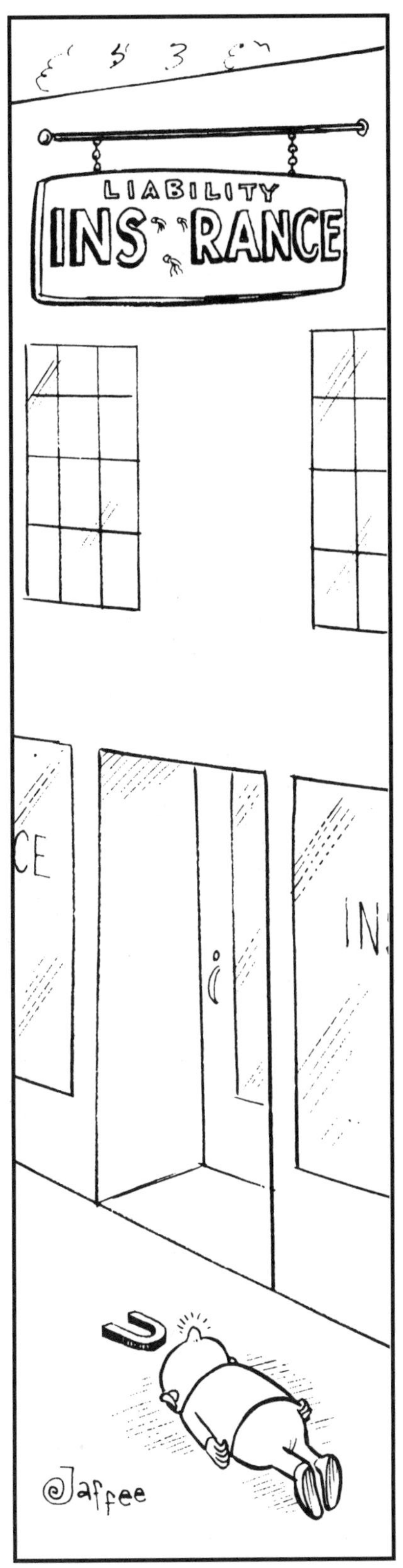
LIABILITY
INS RANCE
CE
INS
©Jaffee

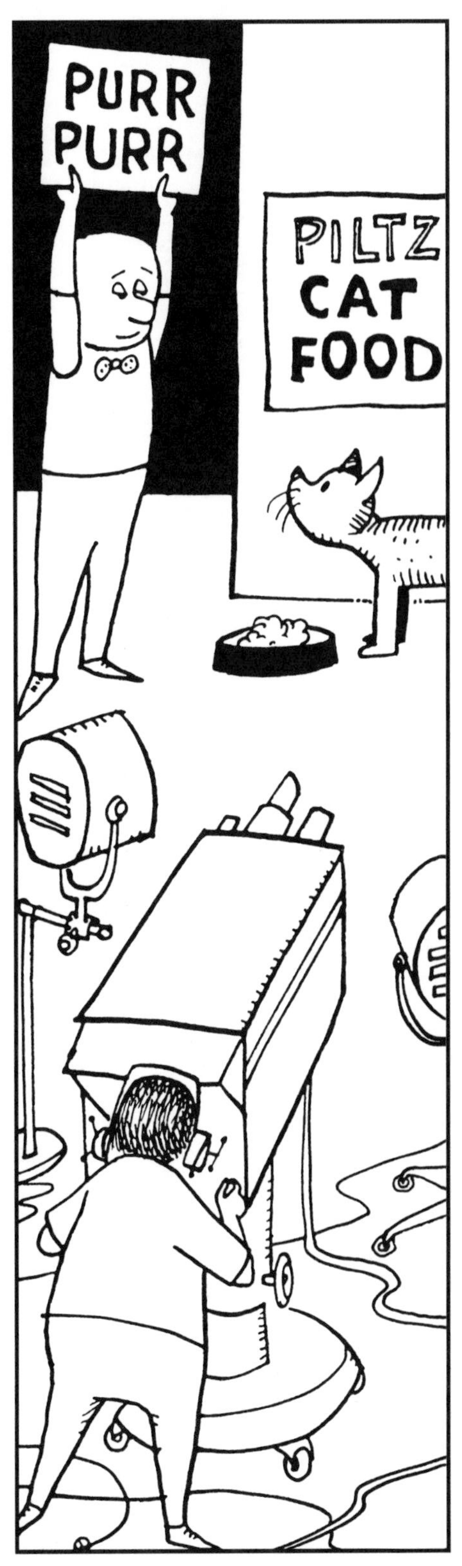
PURR
PURR
PILTZ
CAT
FOOD

Jaffee

DANGER
Jaffee

KNOT
TYING
Jaffe

SUGGESTION
BOX

OUT
IN
Jaffee

EXPRESS
ELEVATOR

BALLOONS
10¢
Jaffee

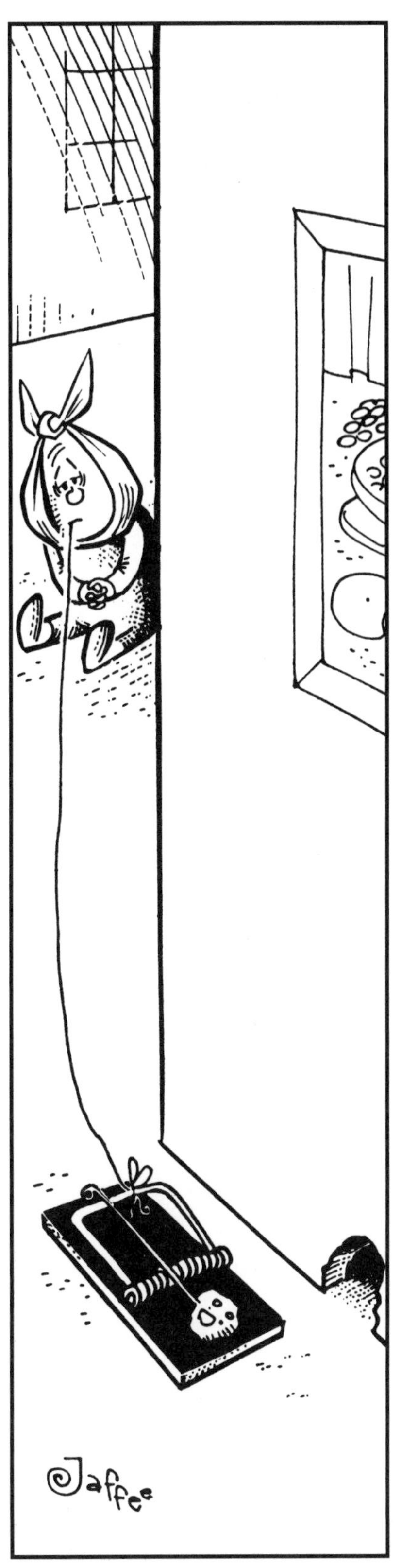
©Jaffee

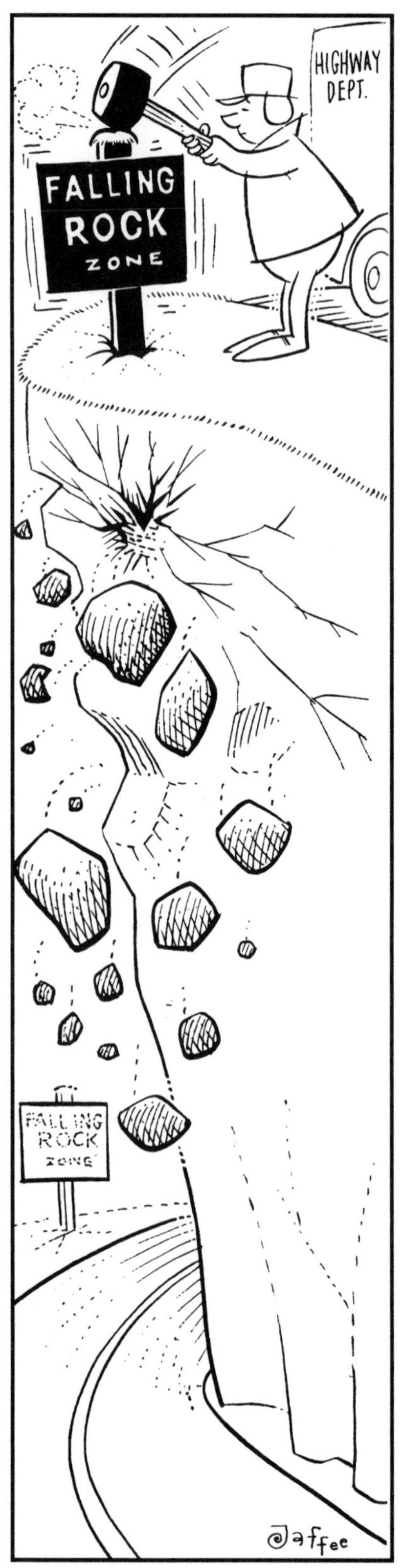
HIGHWAY
DEPT.
FALLING
ROCK
ZONE
FALLING
ROCK
ZONE
Jaffee

6-9
X
IX
VIII
VII
VI
V
IV
III
Jaffee

Jaffee

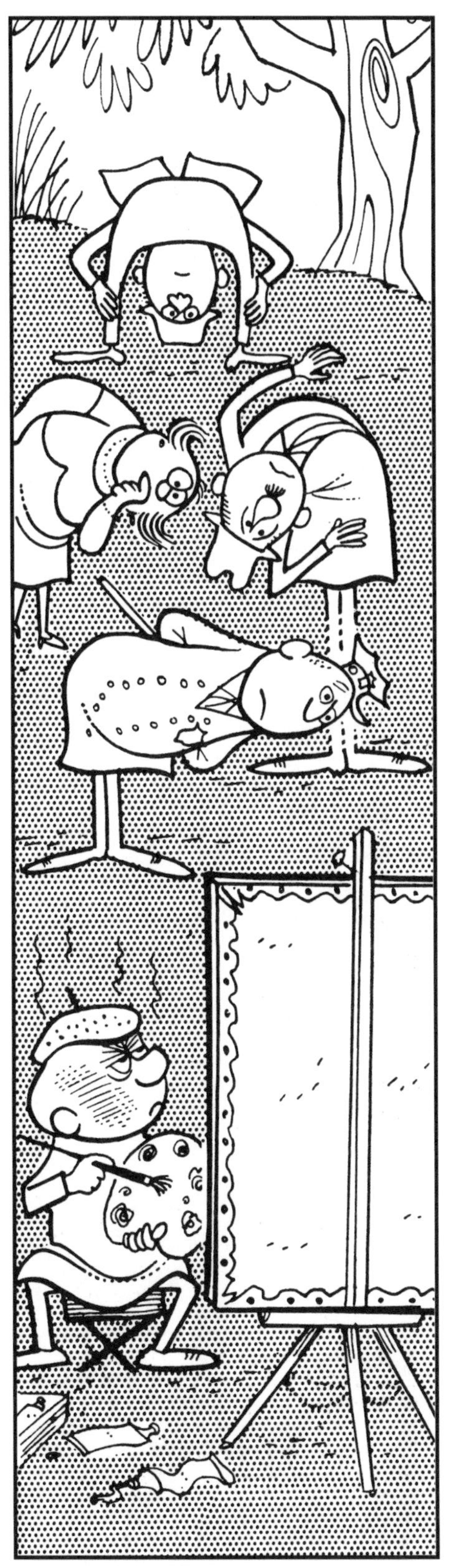

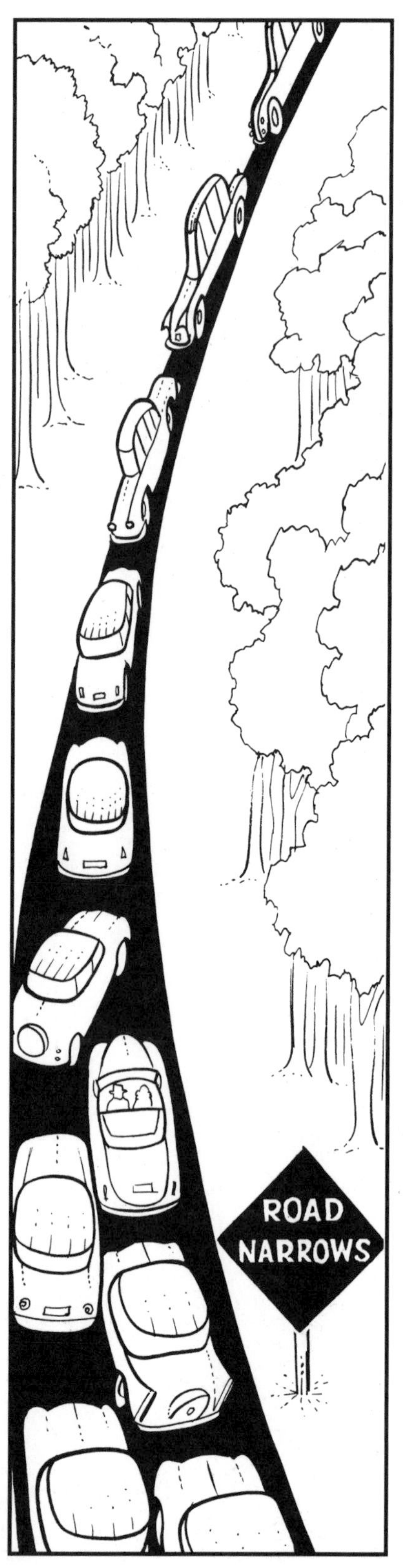
ROAD
NARROWS

Jaffee

FRESH
SEAFOOD
Jaffee

Jaffee

Jaffee

SNEATH'S RETREAT
PRIVATE BEACH KEEP OFF
Jaffee

THE
GREAT
MOUSTACHIO
Jafpee

THE
HUMAN CANNONBALL

WITHDRAWALS
DEPOSITS
Jaffee

©Jaffee

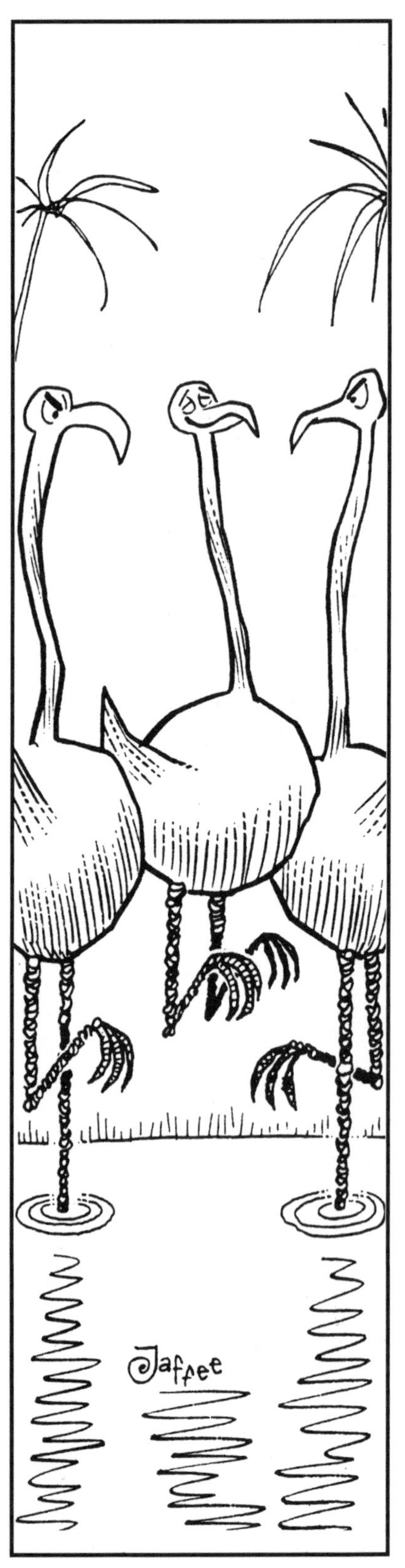
Jaffee

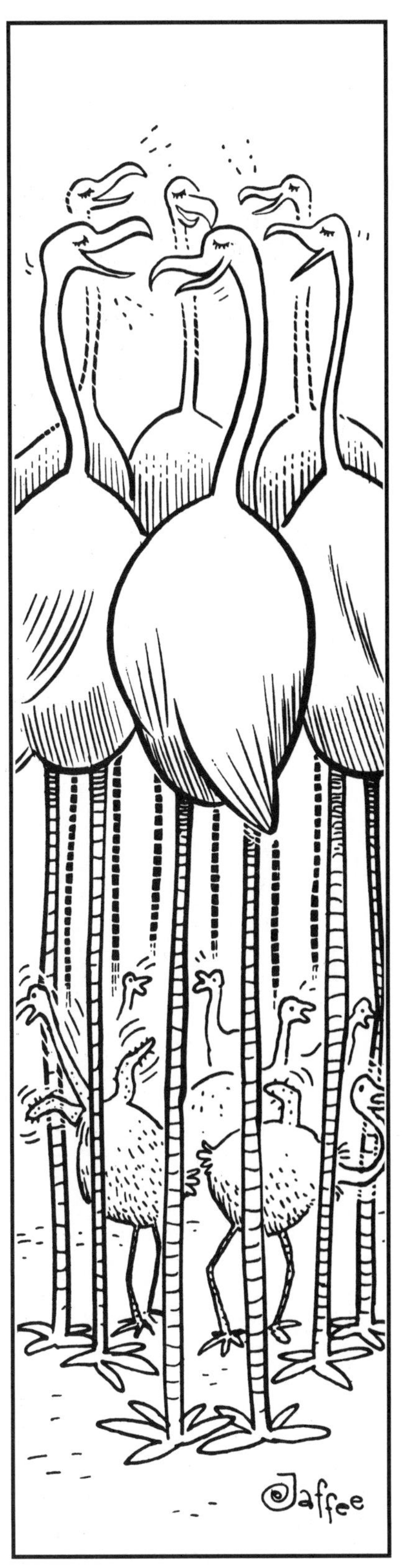
Jaffee

Jaffee

ECHO
MOUNTAIN
Jaffee

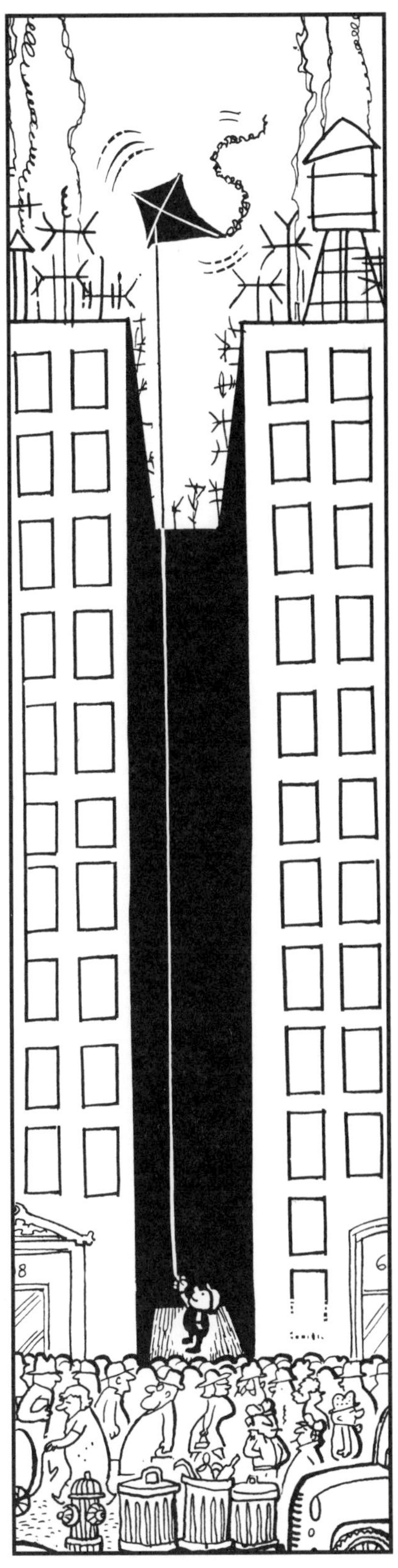

FRESH
MILK
SIDNEY
Jaffee

Madame Avoirdupois
REDUCING
SALON
ENTRANCE
EXIT
SID

3
75
11
29
4
60432
7
38
5
12
9
Jaffee

SCHOOL
CROSSING
Jaffee

Jaffee

HOSPITAL
QUIET
BANG
COACH

TAXI
OFF DUTY
Jaffee

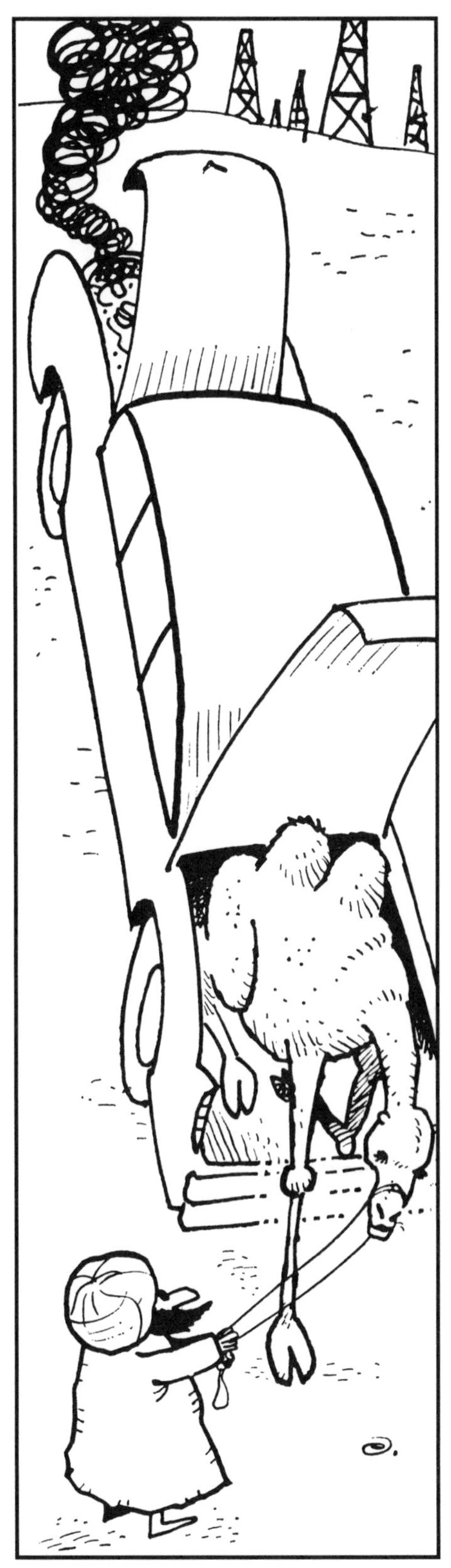

Jaffee

Jaffee

Jaffee

©Jaffee

Jaffee

THE
GREAT
SIDNEY
Jaffee

INDIA
RUBBER
MAN
& FAMILY
0246
Jaffee

WARDEN
HART

Jaffee

MILITARY HERO'S
CLUB

8th ANNUAL
BOARD MEETING
NATIONAL
TRICK CIGAR
COMPANY

Jaffee

LADIES' MASSAGE SALON
DOCTOR JONES
EAT AT ED'S
206
MAIN ST
SIDNEY
Jaffee

Jaffee

S.S. P. KUZMA
Jaffee

Jaffee

AIRLINES
Jaffee

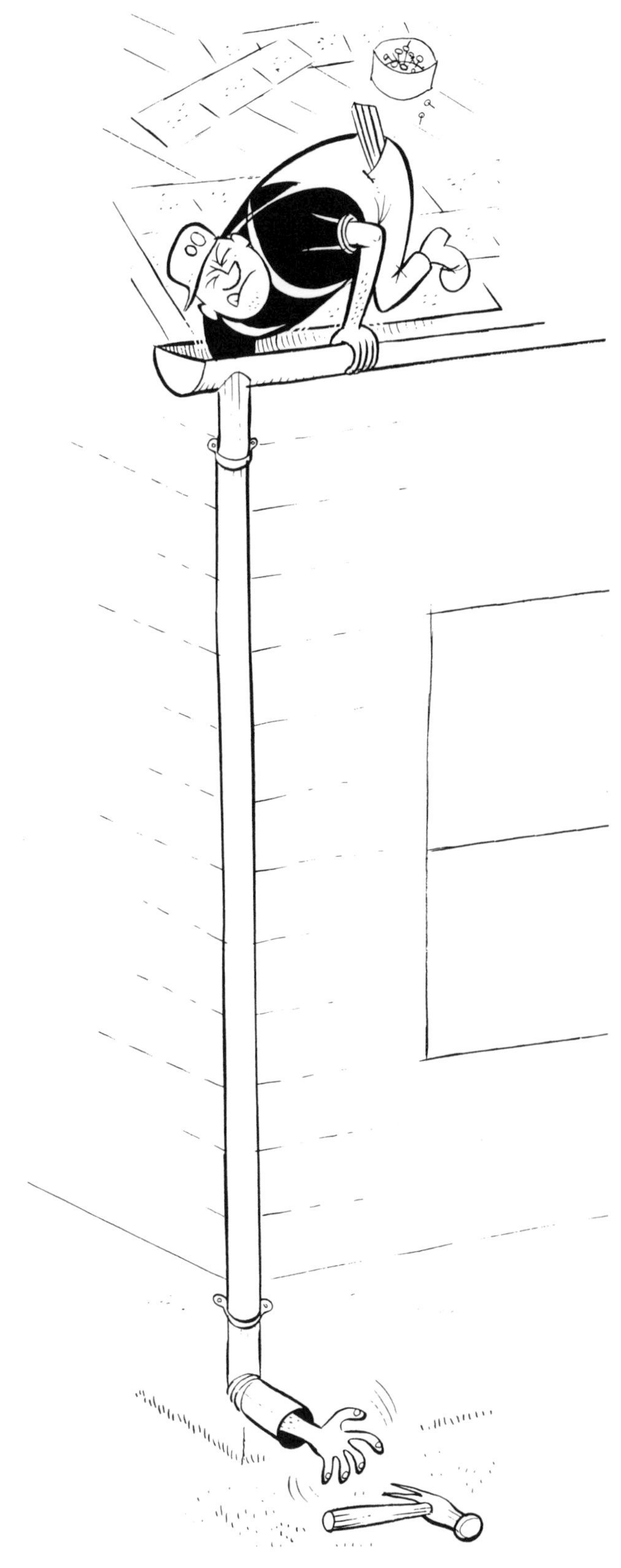

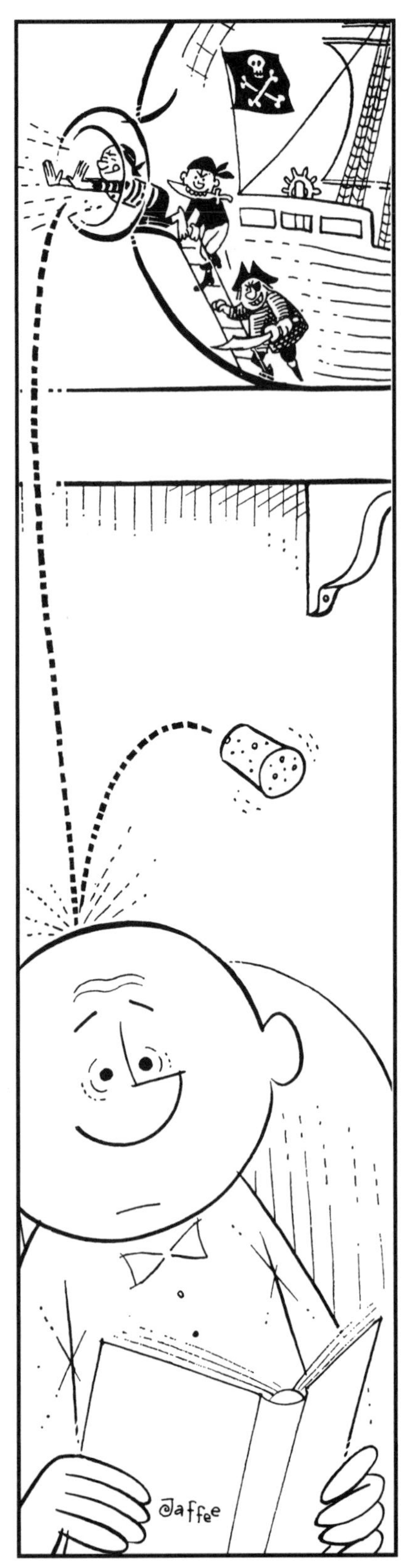
Jaffee

MD.
M.D.
Jaffee

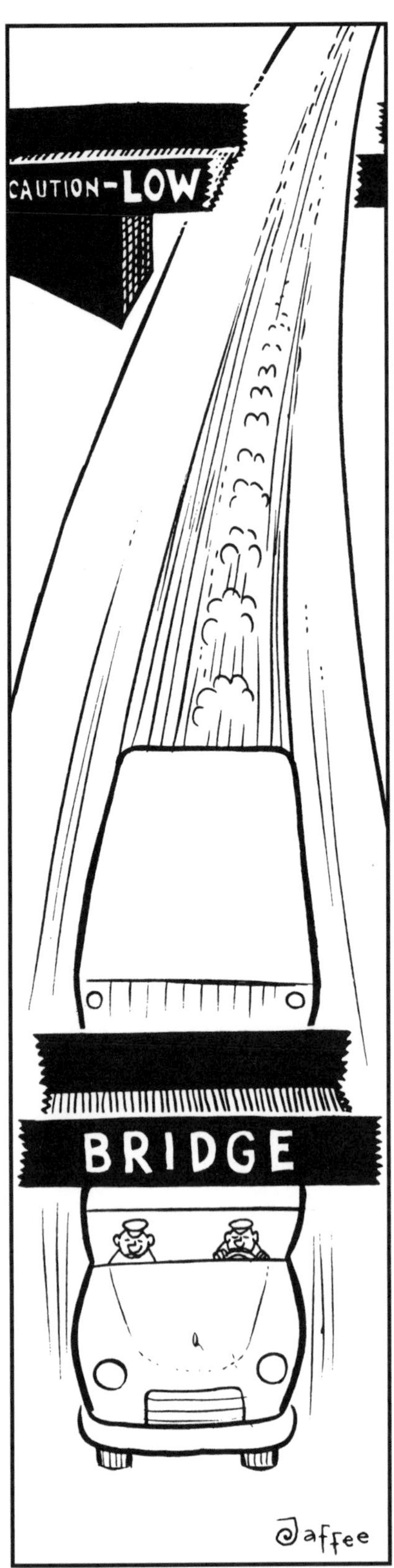
CAUTION-LOW
BRIDGE
Jaffee

Jaffee

BUY
SALE
Jaffee

DRIVING
SCHOOL

Jaffee

PEG-LEG
PETE'S
PLACE
Jaffee

Jaffee

Jaffee

MISS
UNIVERSE
CONTEST
MISS SWEDEN
MISS SPAIN
MISS U.S.A.
Jaffee

CLUB
ALADDIN

KEEP OFF
THE GRASS
Jaffee

©Jaffee

LOVE BIRDS
©Jaffee

©Jaffee

P
Y
W
T
Jaffee

PHYSICS
LAB
Jaffee

HELP

HELP

SIDNEY
SNEATH
DANCE
STUDIO
©Jaffee

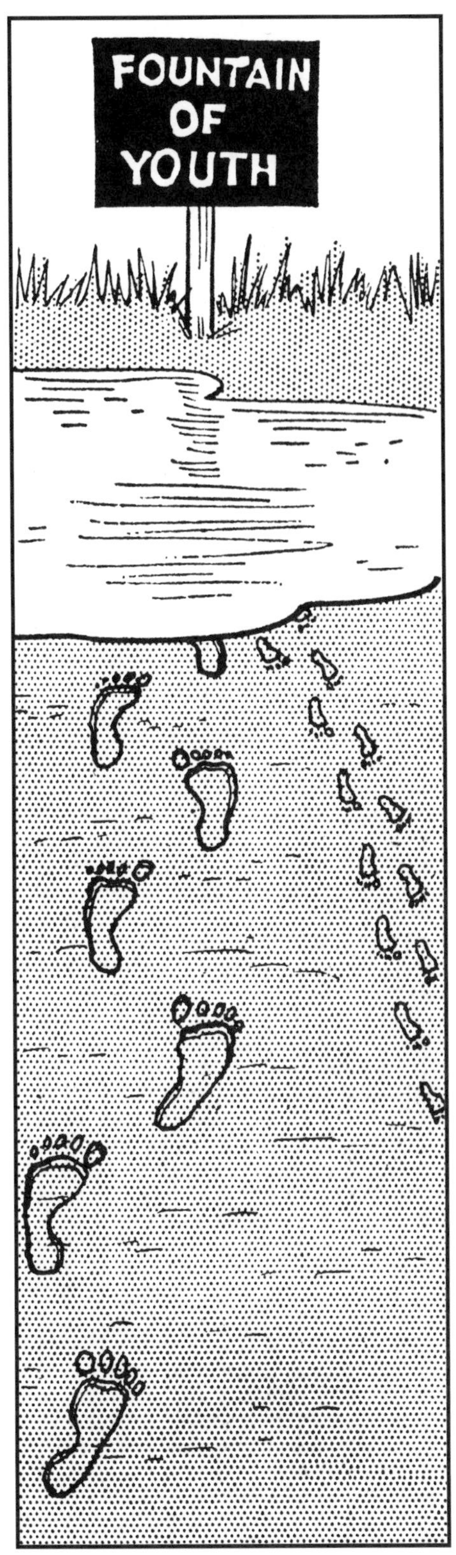
FOUNTAIN
OF
YOUTH

GIVE
GIVE
GET
Jaffee

HAND LETTERED
SLOGANS
THINK
THINK
THINK
THINK
Jaffee

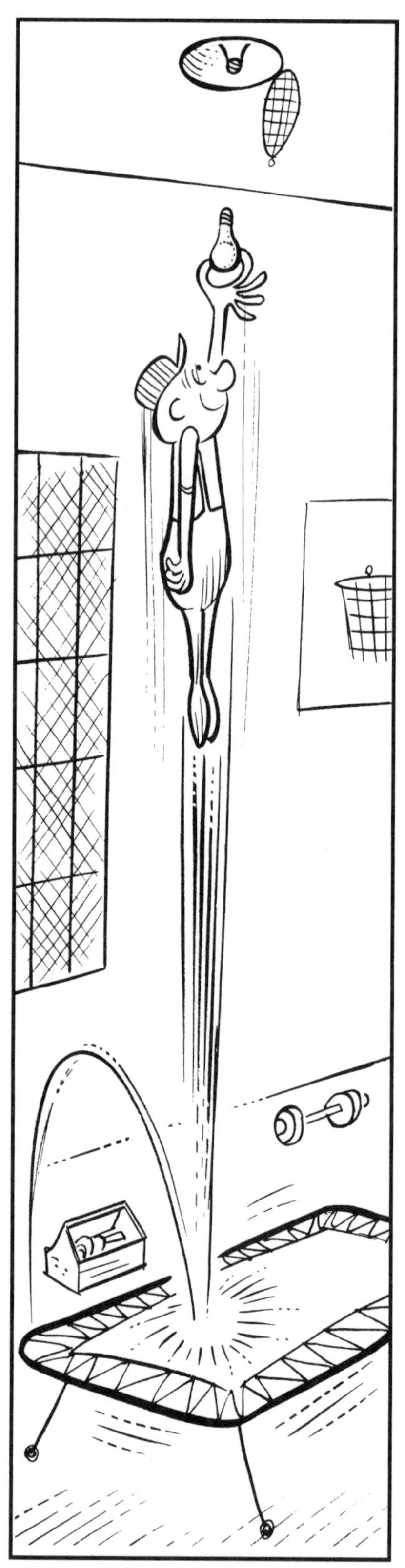

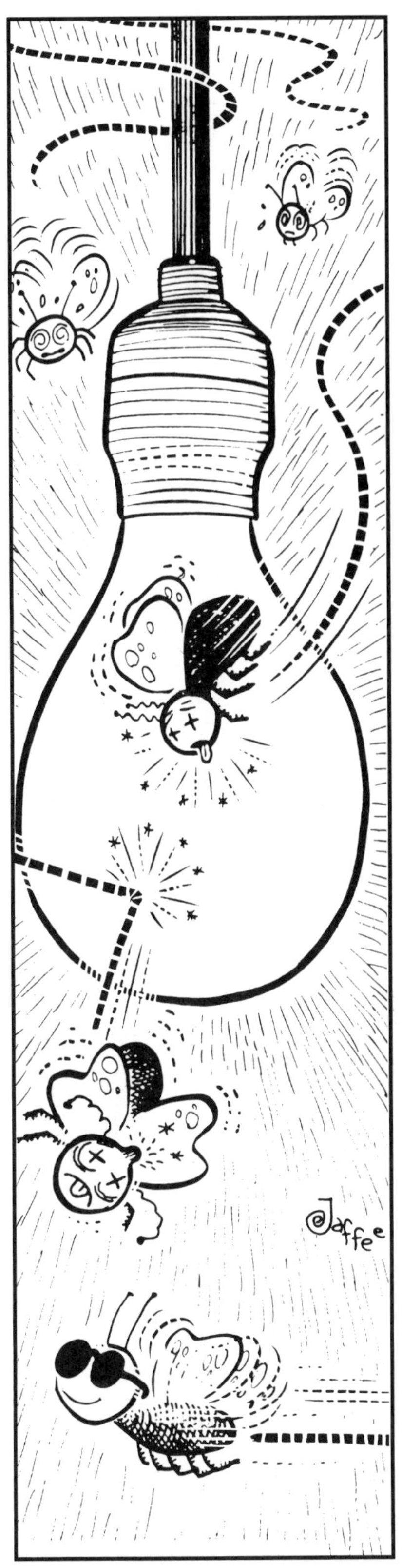
Jaffee

Jaffee

HOTEL
Jaffee

N S

Jaffee